The life cycle of an
Owl

Ruth Thomson

WAYLAND

D1486132

First published in 2008 by Wayland,
a division of Hachette Children's Books

Copyright © Wayland 2008

Wayland
338 Euston Road
London NW1 3BH

Wayland Australia
Level 17/207 Kent Street
Sydney, NSW 2000

All rights reserved

Editor: Clare Lewis
Designer: Simon Morse
Consultant: David Ramsden, Senior Conservation Officer,
The Barn Owl Trust

Photographs: 7 Birdman Photographer/Alamy;
20-21, 23 (br) Michael Callan/Frank Lane Picture Agency;
cover (cr), 12, 23 (tr) DK Limited/Kim Taylor/Corbis: COVER
(cr); Cover (main) Val Duncan/Kenebec Images/Alamy;
8 Lisa Moore/Alamy; 18 Michael Roas/Frank Lane Picture
Agency; 14 Michael Leech/OSF/Photolibrary Group;
3, 4, 5, 6, 7, 9, 10, 11, 13, 15, 16, 17, 19, 22
naturepl.com

British Library Cataloguing in Publication Data
Thomson, Ruth
    The life cycle of an owl. - (Learning about life cycles)
    1. Owls - Life cycles - Juvenile literature
    I. Title
    598.9'7156
ISBN-13: 978-0-7502-5594-3

Printed and bound in China

Wayland is a division of Hachette Children's
Books, an Hachette Livre UK company
www.hachettelivre.co.uk

Contents

Owls live here

This owl lives near farms and grassland. At dawn and dusk, it glides low over fields in search of mice, shrews and **voles**.

What is an owl?

An owl is a bird of **prey**. This means it hunts small animals for food. It has very good eyesight and hearing. It flies silently and pounces on animals with its feet. It usually swallows them whole.

There are many types of owl.
This book is about a barn owl.

large head that can turn right around and upside-down

disc of flat feathers which direct sounds to the ears

soft, fringed feathers for quiet flight

large round eyes that help the owl to see in dim light

hooked beak for tearing up food

sharp, curved **claws** for gripping prey

Finding a mate

In spring, males and females **roost** near the nest. The male offers food to the female to make her plump before they **mate**.

The pair chase around, **screeching** loudly. They also **preen** each other and rub cheeks.

Laying eggs

The female lays her eggs on a soft layer of **pellets**. She lays between three and seven eggs. These are laid two days apart.

The mother sits on her eggs
to keep them warm. She turns
them from time to time. The
male brings her food to eat.

Hatching

After a month, the chicks **hatch**, one every two days. They scrape the eggshell until it cracks open. They push their way out.

Owl chicks are blind and weak.
They are covered with only
a thin coat of fluffy **down**.

2 days

Chicks

The chicks stay near their mother to keep warm.

1 week

The father brings food for them all.
The mother tears it into small
pieces and feeds the chicks.
They grow a thicker fluffy coat.

3
weeks

Owlets

The owlets get bigger and stronger. They begin to run and practise pouncing.

5 weeks

Feathers start to grow on the owlets' wings.

8 weeks

9 weeks

Soon, they are feathered all over. They practise flapping their wings.

10 weeks

Time to fly

Now the owlets are strong enough to fly. At first, they take short flights.

Once the owlets can fly well, they hunt for their own food. They **roost** in nearby trees.

12
weeks

Leaving home

There is not enough food to feed the whole family in the same area. The owlets have to fly away.

14 weeks

They often travel
many miles before
they find a new
place to **roost**
and hunt.

1
year

Adult owl

Now the owl is fully grown.
In spring, it will find a **mate**
and produce young of its own.

22

Owl life cycle

Eggs
The female lays
three to seven eggs,
one every two days.

Chicks
The chicks **hatch**
one at a time.

Adult owls
The adult owls find a **mate**
and produce young of
their own.

Owlets
The owlets grow feathers and learn
to fly. They leave their parents and
find a home of their own.

Glossary

claw a curved, pointed nail at the end of a bird or animal's foot

down the light, soft feathers of chicks

hatch to come out of an egg

mate when a male and female join together to produce young

pellet a small hard ball, which contains the bones and fur of the animals the owl has eaten. It comes out of the owl's beak.

preen when a bird smooths and cleans its feathers

prey the creatures that a bird or an animal hunts for food

roost to sleep

screech to make a loud, harsh cry

vole a small furry animal similar to a mouse

Index

24